involves no precooking or marinating. The ingredients are simply added to the hot oil and turned and tossed over moderately high heat until ready.

● The second method is known in China as *bao* which means 'to explode'. Intense heat is used for this technique, in which foods cut to the same size (and precooked if necessary by steaming or boiling) are cooked very rapidly for a short time, often with the addition of sugar, sherry or vinegar, soy sauce or other flavourings.

● The final method is sometimes known as stir braising. Ingredients such as meat (or fish) and vegetables are ˌ ˌ ˌ ed separatelˌ ˌ ˌ ˌ ˌ ˌ ned with stock ˌ ˌ ˌ ˌ king ˌ ˌ ˌ ˌ ˌ ˌ ˌ ˌ more ˌ ˌ ˌ ˌ ˌ ˌan ˌ ˌ ˌ ˌtional pan. ˌ ˌ ˌ ˌedients – sherry, ˌ ˌ ˌ and cornflour is a ˌ ˌ ˌ ar combination – are often added to rapidly cooked stir fries towards the end of cooking. It is not necessary to remove the ingredients already in the wok; simply push them to the sides and add the sauce to the centre, combining it with the other ingredients once it has come to the boil and thickened.

The wok, particularly the Cantonese type, can also be used for deep frying, but it is vital that the utensil is stable. Use a metal stand if necessary. You will need less oil than when using a conventional deep fryer, and the wok need not be preheated before the oil is added.

A wok also makes an excellent steamer. It can be used with a bamboo stacking steamer, or the food can be placed directly on a rack over boiling water. Improvise with a cake stand if you do not have a rack for your wok, or place a plate on a metal trivet in the wok. Cover with a high-domed lid, and top up the water level in the wok from time to time if necessary. Aromatic herbs may be added to the water if liked.

moderate heat for about a minute, and then add the oil in a 'necklace' just below the inner rim, so that it runs down to the base. Heat the oil before adding the first batch of ingredients. This prevents items from sticking and, because the oil is hot, it will seal the food swiftly, which prevents too much oil from being absorbed.

The best medium for stir frying is groundnut oil, since it can be heated to a high temperature without smoking. Sunflower or safflower oil may be used instead. Corn oil can also be heated to a high temperature without smoking, but does impart a subtle flavour to the food, as does rapeseed oil. Sesame oil is much prized for its nutty flavour, but burns readily; it is, however, frequently combined with other oils and is an important ingredient in the specially formulated stir-fry oils that are now

available.

Ingredients such as garlic or ginger are sometimes used to flavour the oil at the start of cooking. Watch these carefully and keep the heat moderately low, as they burn easily. Once their job has been done, such flavourings can be removed with a slotted spoon, and the temperature raised before the main ingredients are added.

Always add the ingredients in the order listed in recipes. The times indicated are there as a guide; you will soon learn which ingredients need slightly longer than others, so that should you choose to substitute one ingredient for another, you will know at which stage to add it.

There are three basic ways of stir frying:

● The simplest method, used extensively for vegetables,

MEAT DISHES IN MINUTES

A small amount of meat goes a long way in a stir fry. Buy the best quality you can afford, cut it against the grain, and you will be rewarded with a beautifully tender dish that takes little time to cook.

Crunchy Pork and Vegetable Stir Fry

2 tblspn oil

500g (1lb) pork fillet, cut in thin strips

1 tblspn grated fresh root ginger

2 spring onions, finely sliced

2 cloves garlic, crushed

1/4 tspn chilli powder

125g (4oz) drained canned baby sweetcorn

1 large carrot, cut in very thin strips

90g (3oz) small cauliflower florets, blanched, then drained

90g (3oz) frozen peas, thawed

125g (4oz) green beans, topped and tailed

60g (2oz) peanuts

60ml (2fl oz) chicken stock

1 tblspn soy sauce

2 tspn clear honey

2 tspn cornflour dissolved in l tblspn cold water

1 tblspn chopped fresh coriander

1 Preheat wok, then add oil. When hot, add pork, ginger, spring onions, garlic and chilli powder. Stir fry over high heat for 3-4 minutes. Transfer pork to a bowl.

2 Add vegetables and nuts to wok and stir fry for 2 minutes. Transfer to bowl with pork.

3 Add stock, soy sauce, honey and cornflour mixture to wok. Stir constantly until mixture boils and thickens. Return pork and vegetables to wok and cook until heated. Garnish with coriander.
Serves 4

Fillet of Pork with Star Anise

125g (4oz) small shallots, peeled but left whole

2 tblspn oil

1 clove garlic, peeled

2 star anise

500g (1lb) pork fillet, cut in thin strips

2 sticks celery, diagonally sliced

1 tspn drained green peppercorns

185ml (6fl oz) chicken stock

2 tspn cornflour dissolved in 1 tblspn cold water

1 tblspn rice wine or pale dry sherry

1 Put shallots in a small saucepan with water to cover. Bring to the boil, turn off the heat and leave to stand for 5 minutes. Drain and pat dry with paper towels. Set aside.

2 Preheat wok, then add oil. Heat gently, then add garlic and star anise and stir fry for 1 minute. Discard garlic and star anise.

3 Raise heat, add pork to wok and stir fry over high heat for 3-4 minutes. Transfer pork to a bowl and set aside.

4 Add shallots and celery to wok and stir fry for 2 minutes. Return pork to wok and add green peppercorns, stock, cornflour mixture and rice wine or sherry. Bring to the boil and cook, stirring, until thickened.
Serves 4

Fillet of Pork with Star Anise (top), Crunchy Pork and Vegetable Stir Fry

SPICY WOK Cooking

There can be few pieces of kitchen equipment as versatile as the wok. What other utensil can be used for stir frying, simmering, braising, steaming or deep frying, requiring only one gas flame or hot plate to produce dishes that range from simple vegetable accompaniments to complex one-pot meals?

Woks are for everyone, from the student with limited cooking facilities, to the busy parent trying to feed the family a nutritious meal in the shortest possible time and at reasonable cost. Stir fries score on all fronts as they tend to use more vegetables than meat or fish (and more green vegetables than starchy ones), and the rapid cooking means less loss of nutrients and little absorption of fat.

Woks save on washing up, too. You can serve straight from your wok and, if it is properly seasoned, it will only require a quick hot wash and thorough drying before being put away ready for the next time you choose to use it – which should be soon; too many woks gather dust on shelves or remain packed away in boxes because their owners save them for a once-a-month special stir fry.

The recipes can – and should – be adapted to suit your own tastes and the availability of fresh produce. The important thing to remember is to choose substitutes with similar texture and flavour, cutting them to about the same size as the other ingredients.

CONTENTS

WOK KNOW-HOW	2
MEAT DISHES IN MINUTES	4
CHICKEN IN THE WOK	16
QUICK FISH DISHES FROM THE WOK	24
STIR FRIES WITHOUT MEAT	29
RICE AND NOODLE ACCOMPANIMENTS	41
MENUS FOR WOK MEALS	46
GLOSSARY	47
INDEX	48

WOK KNOW-HOW

Woks come in a range of materials, including cast iron and stainless steel, but by far the best is the simple carbon steel type on sale in Oriental markets or shops.

There's no point in buying a small wok. You can stir fry a single shrimp in a large wok but put large quantities of food in a small wok and you won't be able to turn them successfully. The optimum size is 26cm (14in), which gives ample room to cook for a family of four.

There are basically two styles of wok available: the pau wok, which has a single handle and which is specifically designed for stir frying, and the twin-handled Cantonese wok, which is more generally used for steaming and deep frying. Whichever type you buy, make sure the wok has wooden handles for safe handling.

Electric woks, woks with nonstick finishes, and boxed sets are all available, but you may find that a simple pau wok is adequate for your needs.

Accessories

Few special accessories are required for wok cookery. A long-handled metal turner, curved to the shape of the wok, is very useful, but beginners can easily make do with a spatula. Similarly, you can buy brass wire skimmers for draining deep-fried items, but a slotted spoon works just as well. Some cooks like to use the traditional stiff split bamboo brushes to clean their woks after use, but an ordinary plastic kitchen brush is as effective. Most woks come with a half or full rack for steaming small items; however, if you want to be able to steam a number of dishes simultaneously you will need to invest in a stacking bamboo steamer.

For food preparation, you will need a good selection of sharp knives. Most experienced wok cooks wouldn't be without a cleaver. These miniature choppers may look like offensive weapons, but they are marvellous for slicing meats, cutting up vegetables, and even crushing garlic and ginger, with the added bonus that you can use the large flat surface to convey the food to bowl or wok. Buy a good quality cleaver, treat it with respect and store it safely out of the reach of children.

Care of the Wok

If your new wok has a protective oil coating, remove this before using the wok for the first time. Scrub the wok, if necessary, using hot water and a non-abrasive cleanser. Dry the wok, then season it as follows: Heat the wok gently until it is hot and completely dry, then remove from the heat and rub the inside all over with a wad of paper towel dipped in oil. At first the paper will turn black, but eventually it will stay clean. At this stage the wok will be ready for use. A seasoned wok only needs washing in hot water and thorough drying after use, but if you do have to resort to scrubbing it, don't worry. After each use, coat the inside of your wok with a thin layer of oil to prevent it from rusting.

Fuel

You can use a wok with gas, electricity or solid fuel appliances. It is generally felt that gas is the best fuel, as the design of the hob means that the wok sits snugly over the flame. Some woks come with stands for use on solid hotplates, but these are not very successful. It is better to look out for the flat-bottomed woks designed specifically for electric and solid fuel stoves.

Preparation

Before tackling any wok recipe for the first time, read it through to establish the order of work, and assemble all the ingredients next to the cooker. It is a good idea to take a leaf out of the TV cook's book, and have everything laid out in order of use, with any sauce mixtures ready mixed in jugs, and items such as chopped herbs in small bowls. Even something as simple as measuring a tablespoon of soy sauce can slow you down when you are cooking a meal in a wok, so get it ready in advance.

The most time-consuming part of wok cookery is the preparation. It is important that the food is cut into small pieces of uniform size, so that they will cook quickly and evenly. Careful preparation also improves the appearance of the finished dish, so it is worthwhile spending some time mastering the techniques of chopping and slicing. Meats, mushrooms and leaf vegetables are generally sliced across the grain, while celery, Chinese cabbage and spring onions are usually sliced diagonally. When a recipe calls for julienne vegetables, very thin matchstick strips are required. To cut a root vegetable such as parsnip or carrot into julienne strips, first square off the sides of the peeled and trimmed vegetable, then cut it neatly into rectangles. Stack the rectangles on top of each other and cut each rectangle neatly into very thin strips. The stacked strips can then be cut to the required length.

Cooking

The preliminaries – preheating the empty wok and adding the oil – are very important. Never start cooking in a cold wok. Set it over

Chinese Ginger Beef

1 tspn cornflour
60ml (2fl oz) chicken stock
finely chopped root ginger,
1/4 tsp chilli powder
60ml (2fl oz) rice wine or pale dry sherry
1 tblspn brown sugar
500g (1lb) lean sirloin steak, cut in thin 5cm (2in) strips
1 tblspn oil
1 small Chinese cabbage, shredded

1 Combine cornflour and stock. Add ginger, chilli powder, rice wine or sherry and sugar and pour into a large shallow dish. Add beef strips, toss to coat, then cover and marinate for 1 hour at room temperature. Drain beef, reserving marinade.

2 Preheat wok, then add oil. When hot, add beef and stir fry over high heat for 2 minutes. Add cabbage and stir fry for 1 minute, push meat and cabbage to the sides of wok and add marinade to centre. When marinade boils and thickens, toss with other ingredients for 1 minute.
Serves 4

Beef in Black Bean Sauce

1 tspn cornflour dissolved in l tblspn water
1 tblspn black bean sauce
1 tblspn soy sauce
3 tblspn beef stock
1 tspn sugar
1 tblspn oil
1 clove garlic, halved
1 tspn finely chopped fresh root ginger
375g (12oz) lean rump steak, cut in thin strips
2 tspn sesame oil
1 leek, finely sliced
1/2 red pepper, sliced
90g (3oz) beansprouts
60g (2oz) mangetout

1 Combine cornflour mixture, black bean sauce, soy sauce, stock and sugar in a jug. Mix well.

2 Preheat wok, then add oil. When moderately hot, add garlic and ginger. Stir fry for 1 minute, then remove garlic.

3 Raise heat, add steak to wok and stir fry for 3 minutes. Remove and set aside.

4 Add sesame oil to wok. When hot, stir fry leek, red pepper, beansprouts and mangetout for 2-3 minutes.

5 Push vegetables to sides of wok and add cornflour mixture to centre. Cook, stirring, until mixture thickens slightly. Combine with vegetables. Return beef to wok, and cook for 2-3 minutes.
Serves 4

Chinese Beef Stir Fry

1 clove garlic, crushed
1 tblspn cornflour dissolved in 2 tblspn soy sauce
500g (1lb) beef fillet, cut in 5mm (1/4in) slices
2 tblspn oil
3 sticks celery, thinly sliced
1 small carrot, sliced in thin rounds
1 tblspn tomato sauce
1 tspn Worcestershire sauce
2 tblspn chicken stock
2 tblspn hoisin sauce

1 Combine garlic and cornflour mixture in a large shallow dish. Add beef slices and stir until well coated. Cover and allow to stand for 20 minutes.

2 Preheat wok, then add oil. When hot, add beef and stir fry over high heat for 1 minute.

3 Add celery and carrot and stir fry for 2-3 minutes. Remove beef mixture from wok and set aside.

Sweet and Sour Meatballs (top), Chinese Beef Stir Fry

4 Add remaining ingredients to wok and stir over high heat until sauce boils and thickens. Return beef mixture and toss in sauce until heated through.

Serves 4

Sweet and Sour Meatballs

1 x 440g (14oz) can pineapple chunks
1 tblspn cornflour
1 tblspn soy sauce
1 tblspn wine vinegar
2 tblspn brown sugar
500g (1lb) minced steak
2 spring onions, finely sliced
2 tblspn plum sauce or sweet fruit chutney
flour
3 tblspn oil
1 small onion, finely chopped
1 green pepper, finely chopped

1 Drain pineapple chunks, reserving 125ml (4fl oz) of juice. Add cornflour, soy sauce, vinegar and brown sugar and mix well.

2 Combine steak, spring onions and plum sauce or chutney in a bowl. Mix well. Form into 20 small meatballs. Roll meatballs in flour to coat.

3 Preheat wok, then heat 2 tbspn of oil. Add meatballs a few at a time and fry, turning frequently, for 10-15 minutes or until cooked. Remove meatballs and drain on paper towels.

4 Heat oil in wok. Add onion and green pepper and stir fry for 3 minutes over high heat.

5 Push vegetables to sides of wok, add pineapple chunks and cornflour mixture to centre and bring to the boil, stirring until the mixture thickens. Toss with vegetables. Return meatballs to wok, cover and simmer for 2 minutes or until heated.

Serves 4

Lamb Stir Fry with Walnuts

60ml (2fl oz) light soy sauce

2 tspn sesame oil

1 tblspn vinegar

1 tblspn cornflour

2 tspn brown sugar

2 tblspn groundnut or sunflower oil

750g (1¹/2lb) lamb fillet, cut into thin strips

2.5cm (1in) piece fresh root ginger, peeled and thinly sliced

1 red pepper, cut into thin strips

1 yellow pepper, cut into thin strips

1 large bunch spring onions, diagonally sliced

125g (4oz) walnuts, chopped

1 Combine soy sauce, sesame oil, vinegar, cornflour and brown sugar. Set aside.

2 Preheat wok, heat groundnut or sunflower oil. Add lamb and stir fry over high heat for 2 minutes. Transfer lamb to a bowl.

3 Add ginger to wok with peppers and stir fry for 3 minutes. Add spring onions and stir fry for 1 minute.

4 Push vegetables to sides of wok, add soy sauce mixture to centre and bring to the boil, stirring until sauce thickens. Toss with vegetables. Return lamb to wok with walnuts, toss and cook until heated.
Serves 6

Honey Pork with Vegetable Strips

4 tblspn clear honey

2 tblspn light soy sauce

2 tblspn Worcestershire sauce

375g (12oz) pork fillet, cut in thin strips

2 courgettes, cut in thin strips

1 cucumber, cut in thin strips

1 red pepper, cut in thin strips

2 tblspn oil

1 tspn sesame seeds

1 Combine the honey, soy sauce and Worcestershire sauce in a large shallow dish. Add the pork strips and stir until well coated. Allow to stand for 20 minutes.

2 Meanwhile arrange the courgettes, cucumber and red pepper decoratively around the rim of a large plate.

3 Drain pork and reserve marinade. Preheat wok, then add oil. When hot, add pork strips and stir fry for 3 minutes. Add reserved marinade and cook for 1 minute more, stirring to coat the pork strips in the sauce.

4 Spoon pork mixture into centre of vegetable strips on plate, sprinkle with sesame seeds and serve at once.
Serves 4

Pork and Sage Stir Fry

2 tblspn oil

500g (1lb) pork fillet, cut in thin strips

90g (3oz) Chinese ham or prosciutto, cut in thin strips

1 red pepper, cut in thin strips

¹/2 tspn crushed black peppercorns

1 tblspn chopped fresh sage

1 tblspn hoisin sauce

3 tblspn white wine

2 spring onions, finely sliced

1 Preheat wok, then add oil. When hot, add pork fillet and ham and stir fry for 3-4 minutes. Using a slotted spoon, transfer meat to a bowl and set aside.

2 Reheat oil if necessary. Add red pepper, peppercorns and sage and stir fry for 2 minutes.

3 Stir in hoisin sauce, wine and spring onions and bring to the boil, stirring. Return pork and ham to wok and toss with vegetables and sauce until heated through. Serve at once.
Serves 4

Honey Pork with Vegetable Strips

Stir-fried Pork with Beans and Sesame Seeds

1 tblspn sesame oil

1 tblspn sunflower oil

2 garlic cloves, crushed

500g (1lb) pork fillet, cut in small cubes

375g (12oz) French beans, topped, tailed and cut in half diagonally

1/2 red pepper, finely chopped

1 tspn finely chopped fresh root ginger

2 tblspn sesame seeds

2 tblspn dark soy sauce

2 tspn brown sugar

1 Preheat wok, then add oils. When hot, add garlic and pork and stir fry for 3-4 minutes. Using a slotted spoon, transfer pork and garlic to a bowl and set aside.

2 Reheat oil if necessary, add beans, red pepper and ginger and stir fry for 1 minute over high heat. Return pork and garlic to wok with sesame seeds, soy sauce and brown sugar. Cook, stirring constantly until pork is heated through and glazed. Beans should be bright green and crisp. Serve at once.
Serves 4

Kitchen Tip
Burghul, which is also known as cracked wheat, makes a delicious change from rice. To prepare it, heat 2 tblspn oil in a saucepan, add 250g (8oz) medium-grain burghul and stir until well coated. Add 440ml (14fl oz) water and 1 tspn salt. Bring to the boil, then lower the heat, cover and simmer for 20 minutes. Remove pan from heat, leaving lid on, and set aside in a warm place for 10 minutes. Fluff up grains with fork and serve.
Serves 4

Twice-cooked Pork with Noodles

6 dried Chinese mushrooms

salt

250g (8oz) vermicelli or medium egg noodles

315g (10oz) cold roast pork, sliced into thin strips

4 tblspn hoisin sauce

1 tblspn sunflower oil

1 tspn sesame oil

1 tblspn finely chopped fresh root ginger

1/2 red pepper, cut in thin strips

1/2 yellow pepper, cut in thin strips

125g (4oz) mangetout, topped and tailed

90g (3oz) drained canned bamboo shoots, sliced

2 tblspn clear honey

2 tblspn dark soy sauce

1 tblspn red wine vinegar

1 Soak dried mushrooms in hot water to cover for 20 minutes, drain, remove stems and slice cups thinly. Toss pork strips in hoisin sauce in a shallow dish.

2 Bring a large saucepan of salted water to the boil, add the vermicelli or egg noodles, remove from the heat and allow to stand for about 6 minutes until noodles are tender or *al dente.*

3 Meanwhile, make the stir fry. Preheat wok, then add oils. When hot, add pork strips and sauce, with ginger, peppers and mushrooms. Stir fry over high heat for 2 minutes.

4 Add mangetout and bamboo shoots and stir fry for 2 minutes more. Transfer to a bowl, cover and keep warm.

5 Stir honey, soy sauce and vinegar into wok and bring to the boil, stirring. Drain noodles and toss in the sauce until heated through. Serve immediately, topped with the stir-fried vegetables.
Serves 4

Moroccan Sweet and Spicy Stew

This fruity stew provides ample proof that the wok should not be reserved solely for stir fries.

1 tblspn oil

500g (1lb) stewing steak, cut into 2cm (3/4 in) cubes

8 shallots, peeled but left whole

500ml (16fl oz) beef stock

1 tspn ground cinnamon

2 tblspn clear honey

1/2 tspn grated nutmeg

2 tblspn sultanas

8 no-need-to-soak dried apricots

125ml (4fl oz) orange juice

60g (2oz) blanched almonds

coriander sprig for garnish

1 Preheat wok, then add oil. When hot, add steak cubes and shallots and stir fry over high heat for 2 minutes. Add stock and cinnamon, bring to the boil, then simmer for 10 minutes, stirring occasionally.

2 Stir in the honey, nutmeg, sultanas and apricots. Lower the heat, cover the wok and simmer for 30 minutes, stirring occasionally.

3 Add orange juice and almonds and simmer for 30 minutes more, uncovered. Garnish with coriander and serve hot, surrounded by yellow rice, if liked.
Serves 4

Stir-fried Pork with Beans and Sesame Seeds (top), Moroccan Sweet and Spicy Stew

Glazed Beef Slices with Sesame Seeds

500g (1lb) beef fillet, cut in 2cm (³/₄in) slices

2 tblspn oil

2 cloves garlic, crushed

1 tblspn brown sugar

¹/₂ tsp five spice powder

2 tblspn red wine vinegar

2 tblspn Worcestershire sauce

2 tblspn soy sauce

sesame seeds to garnish

1 Place the beef slices between 2 pieces of heavy-duty plastic wrap and pound with a mallet or rolling pin to a thickness of 5mm (¹/₄in).

2 Preheat wok, then add oil. When hot, add garlic, sugar, five spice powder, vinegar, Worcestershire sauce and soy sauce. Bring to the boil, then simmer for I minute.

3 Add beef slices to wok, turning to coat with sauce. Cook for 1-2 minutes each side or until tender. Remove beef from wok and keep hot.

4 Bring wok juices to the boil, then simmer until sauce thickens. Pour over beef and sprinkle with sesame seeds.
Serves 4

Kitchen Tip
The cleaver that is such an invaluable utensil when preparing meat, poultry and vegetables for stir fries also makes an excellent garlic crusher. Peel the garlic cloves, sprinkle them with a little salt, cut them through once or twice, then use the flat blade of the cleaver to crush them. The blade is wide enough to cover the garlic completely – no more cloves that skid off the chopping board to disappear down the back of the work surface! When the garlic is crushed, use the flat cleaver blade to convey it to the wok.

Peas with Prosciutto and Pinenuts

2 tblspn butter

1 tspn sugar

250g (8oz) frozen peas, thawed

1 tblspn oil

1 clove garlic, crushed

125g (4oz) prosciutto or Chinese ham, cut in short strips

45g (1¹/₂oz) pinenuts

1 Bring a medium saucepan of water to the boil. Stir in the butter and sugar until dissolved, then add the peas. Cook for about 5 minutes or until just tender, drain and reserve.

2 Preheat wok, then add oil. When hot, add garlic, ham and pinenuts. Stir fry over moderate heat for 2 minutes or until pinenuts are golden. Add peas and cook, stirring, until heated through. Serve at once.
Serves 4

Warm Steak Salad with Pawpaw

500g (1lb) fillet steak, trimmed and cut in thin strips

2 tspn finely chopped rosemary

¹/₂ tspn cayenne pepper

2 tblspn oil

1 small pawpaw, peeled and cut in small cubes

1 small bunch curly endive, torn in bite-sized pieces

Dressing

2 tblspn red wine vinegar

salt

freshly ground black pepper

5 tblspn olive oil

1 Make dressing by combining all the ingredients in a screw-topped jar. Close the jar tightly, shake well and set aside.

Peas with Prosciutto and Pinenuts (top); Glazed Beef Slices with Sesame Seeds

2 Sprinkle fillet steak with rosemary and cayenne. Preheat wok, then add oil. When hot, add steak strips and stir fry for 2 minutes over high heat.

3 Using a slotted spoon, transfer steak strips to a bowl. Add pawpaw and dressing and toss lightly. Divide endive between 4 plates, mound beef salad on the centre of each and serve at once.
Serves 4

Heavenly Beef and Vegetables

(Illustrated on pages 44-45)

125ml (4fl oz) water

60ml (2fl oz) soy sauce

2 tblspn clear honey

2 tspn grated fresh root ginger

1 tspn sesame oil

3 cloves garlic, crushed

500g (1lb) beef fillet, cut in strips

2 tblspn sunflower oil

185g (6oz) mushrooms, sliced

1 red pepper, cut in thin strips

8 canned water chestnuts, thinly sliced

100g (3 1/2 oz) mangetout

1 Combine water, soy sauce, honey, ginger, sesame oil and garlic in a large shallow dish. Add beef strips and stir until well coated. Cover and refrigerate for 2 hours. Drain beef strips, reserving marinade.

2 Preheat wok, then add oil. When hot, add beef strips and stir fry over high heat for 2 minutes. Using a slotted spoon, transfer beef strips to a bowl. Set aside.

3 Reheat oil in wok, add mushrooms, pepper, water chestnuts and mangetout and stir fry for 3 minutes over high heat.

4 Add reserved marinade and bring to the boil, stirring until the sauce thickens. Return the beef strips to wok and heat through, stirring. Serve at once.
Serves 4

San Choy Bow

San Choy Bow

1 tblspn sesame oil

1 tblspn sunflower oil

500g (1lb) minced pork

1 tspn caster sugar

1 onion, finely chopped

1 carrot, cut in fine dice

1 tblspn grated fresh root ginger

2 sticks celery, finely chopped

60ml (2fl oz) chicken stock

2 tblspn soy sauce

1 tblspn rice wine or pale dry sherry

2 tspn cornflour

lettuce leaves to serve

1 Preheat wok, then add oils. When hot, add pork and sugar and stir fry for 3 minutes over high heat until the pork is no longer pink. Transfer pork to a bowl and set aside.

2 Pour off all but 1 tbspn of oil from wok. Reheat and add onion, carrot, ginger and celery. Stir fry for 1 minute, then return pork to wok. Add 2 tbspn stock, soy sauce and rice wine or sherry. Cook, stirring for 2 minutes.

3 Mix cornflour with remaining stock and add to wok. Cook, stirring, until mixture thickens. Serve in lettuce leaves as illustrated.
Serves 4

Liver Stir Fry in Tomato Sauce

750g (1¹/₂lb) lambs' liver, skinned, trimmed and cut in thin strips

2 tspn ground coriander

2 tspn ground cumin

1 tspn ground white pepper

2 tblspn chopped fresh parsley

1 tblspn oil

1 onion, finely chopped

2 cloves garlic, crushed

375g (12oz) drained canned chopped tomatoes

1 tblspn tomato puree

60ml (2fl oz) white wine

1 Place liver in a large shallow dish. Sprinkle with coriander, cumin, pepper and 1 tbspn parsley, toss well, cover and refrigerate for 20 minutes.

2 Preheat wok, then add oil. When hot, add liver and stir fry over high heat for 3 minutes until just cooked. Transfer liver to a bowl and keep warm.

3 Reheat oil in wok, add onion and garlic and stir fry for 3 minutes. Stir in tomatoes, tomato puree and wine and simmer mixture, stirring frequently, for 10 minutes.

4 Return liver to wok, stir until heated through, sprinkle with remaining parsley and serve.
Serves 4

Red Cabbage and Beef Stir Fry

375g (12oz) red cabbage, finely shredded

2 oranges, peeled and segmented

2 spring onions, finely sliced

2 tblspn caraway seeds

2 tblspn lemon juice

1 tspn crushed black peppercorns

3 tblspn oil

625g (1¹/₄lb) rump steak, cut in thin strips

1 tblspn clear honey

2 tblspn snipped chives

1 Combine cabbage, orange segments, spring onions, caraway seeds, lemon juice and pepper in a large bowl. Set aside.

2 Preheat wok, then add oil. When hot, add steak strips and honey and stir fry over moderately high heat for 2 minutes.

3 Add the cabbage mixture, toss and cook over high heat for 2 minutes until the cabbage begins to wilt. Stir in chives and serve.
Serves 6

Mango and Beef Stir Fry

Mango and Beef Stir Fry

2 tblspn sesame oil

3 cloves garlic, crushed

1/2 tspn chilli paste

500g (1lb) fillet steak, cut in thin strips

1 tblspn sunflower oil

1 red pepper, cut in thin strips

8 spring onions, diagonally sliced in 3cm (1 1/4in) lengths

1 tblspn dark soy sauce

1 tblspn rice wine or pale dry sherry

1 tspn brown sugar

1 x 440g (14oz) can mango slices, drained, cut in strips

1 Combine sesame oil, garlic and chilli paste in a large shallow dish. Add beef strips and stir until coated. Allow to stand for 20 minutes.

2 Preheat wok, then add sunflower oil. When hot, add the beef and stir fry for 2 minutes. Transfer beef to a bowl and set aside.

3 Reheat the oil in the wok, add red pepper, spring onions, soy sauce, rice wine or sherry and brown sugar and cook, stirring, for 1 minute.

4 Return beef to the wok. Add mango and stir gently, taking care not to break mango flesh.
Serves 4

Stir-fried Beef with Broccoli

500g (1lb) rump steak, cut in thin strips

1 tblspn cornflour dissolved in 1 tblspn light soy sauce

2 tblspn oil

1 clove garlic, crushed

315g (10oz) broccoli stalks, diagonally sliced

90g (3oz) mushrooms, sliced

1 tspn soy sauce

60ml (2fl oz) chicken stock

1 Put the steak strips in a shallow dish, add the cornflour mixture and toss to coat. Set aside.

2 Preheat wok, then add oil. When hot, add garlic and beef strips and stir fry for 3 minutes over moderately high heat. Transfer the beef to a bowl and set aside.

3 Reheat oil in wok, add broccoli and mushrooms and stir fry for 1 minute.

4 Stir in soy sauce and stock, cover the wok and cook over moderate heat for 3-4 minutes. Return beef to wok and toss in sauce until heated.
Serves 4-6

CHICKEN IN THE WOK

Tender, succulent chicken, stripped of its skin and swiftly stir fried with vegetables and flavourings, makes a meal that is as healthy as it is hearty. Most of the recipes in this chapter use boneless chicken breasts, which are low in fat, and require little preparation.

Tasty Chicken with Peas and Pasta

2 tblspn oil
4 boneless chicken breasts, skinned and cut in thin strips
salt
375g (12oz) pasta spirals
250g (8oz) shelled fresh or thawed frozen peas
1 onion, finely chopped
4 tblspn cider vinegar
1 tblspn soy sauce
freshly ground black pepper

1 Preheat wok, then add oil. When hot, add chicken and stir fry for about 3 minutes until just tender. Do not overcook. Using a slotted spoon transfer to a bowl and set aside.

2 Bring a saucepan of lightly salted water to the boil, add the pasta spirals and cook until tender or *al dente*. Cook the peas in a separate pan of boiling water, or in the microwave, for about 4 minutes or until crisp-tender. Drain pasta and peas.

3 Reheat oil in wok. Add onion and vinegar and stir fry over moderate heat for 3-4 minutes until onion is tender. Add pasta, chicken and peas, season with soy sauce and pepper and toss over moderately high heat until heated through. Serve at once.

Serves 4

Chicken in Lettuce

1 Iceberg lettuce
2 tblspn dark soy sauce
1 tblspn sherry
1 tspn caster sugar
250g (8oz) boneless chicken breasts, skinned and cut in thin strips
2 tblspn oil
2 cloves garlic, halved
3 slices fresh root ginger
4 spring onions, diagonally sliced
125g (4oz) mushrooms, sliced
hoisin sauce to serve

1 Separate lettuce into leaves. Select 8 large leaf cups, wash, drain well and dry on paper towels. Refrigerate.

2 Combine soy sauce, sherry and sugar in a shallow dish. Add chicken strips and stir until well coated. Stand for 20 minutes.

3 Preheat wok, then add oil. Heat gently. Add garlic and ginger. Stir fry for 2 minutes. Remove garlic and ginger and discard.

4 Add chicken to oil and stir fry over high heat for 3 minutes. Push chicken to sides of wok, add spring onions and mushrooms and stir fry for 2 minutes.

5 Place chicken mixture in a bowl in the centre of a platter and surround with lettuce cups. Each person spoons a little hoisin sauce into a lettuce cup, adds some chicken mixture, folds lettuce around filling and eats with the fingers.

Serves 4

Stir-fried Chicken with Cashews

Stir-fried Chicken with Cashews

2 tspn cornflour

2 tspn soy sauce

1 tblspn rice wine or pale dry sherry

1/4 tspn sesame oil

2 tblspn sunflower oil

1 red onion, cut in quarters, then separated into petal shapes

1 carrot, diagonally sliced

1 clove garlic, crushed

1 tspn grated fresh root ginger

375g (12oz) boneless chicken breasts, skinned and cut in thin strips

250g (8oz) broccoli, separated into florets

2 tblspn unsalted cashew nuts

125ml (4fl oz) chicken stock

3 spring onions, diagonally sliced

1 Mix cornflour, soy sauce, rice wine or sherry and sesame oil in a small bowl. Set aside.

2 Preheat wok, then add oil. When hot, add onion and carrot and stir fry for 3-4 minutes over high heat. Add garlic and ginger and stir fry for 1 minute more. Using a slotted spoon, transfer vegetables and ginger to a bowl and set aside.

3 Reheat oil in wok and add chicken strips, in batches if necessary. Stir fry for about 3 minutes until just tender. Using slotted spoon, transfer to bowl with vegetable mixture.

4 Add broccoli and cashews to wok and stir fry over moderately high heat for 2 minutes. Push broccoli and cashews to sides of wok and add spring onions with cornflour mixture to centre. Bring to the boil, stirring until mixture thickens. Mix with broccoli and nuts. Return chicken and vegetables to wok and toss until heated through.

Serves 4

Chicken Livers with Ginger

60ml (2fl oz) soy sauce

2 tblspn brandy

1 tspn brown sugar

1 tspn grated fresh root ginger

1 clove garlic, finely chopped

500g (1lb) chicken livers, trimmed

flour

salt

freshly ground black pepper

2 tblspn oil

1 onion, chopped

2 tblspn chopped fresh parsley

1 Mix the soy sauce, brandy, brown sugar, grated ginger and garlic in a jug. Dredge livers in flour, shaking off excess, then sprinkle with salt and pepper and set aside.

2 Preheat wok, then add oil. When hot, add onion and stir fry over high heat for 3 minutes until tender. Add livers and stir fry for 1 minute.

3 Pour soy sauce mixture into wok and cook for about 2 minutes, stirring frequently, until sauce thickens slightly and livers are cooked. Sprinkle with parsley and serve at once.

Serves 4

Indonesian Chicken and Green Beans

3 tblspn oil

4 boneless chicken breasts, skinned and cut in 2cm (3/4in) cubes

250g (8oz) green beans, topped, tailed and cut in 2.5cm (1in) lengths

60ml (2fl oz) lemon juice

2 tblspn soy sauce

1 tblspn brown sugar

2 tspn turmeric

125ml (4fl oz) water

1 Preheat wok, then add oil. When hot, add chicken and stir fry for 3-4 minutes or until cooked. Using a slotted spoon transfer chicken cubes to a bowl and set aside.

2 Reheat oil in wok. Add beans and stir fry for 2 minutes.

3 Stir in lemon juice, soy sauce, brown sugar, turmeric and water. Bring to the boil, then simmer for 3-5 minutes until sauce thickens slightly. Return chicken to the wok and toss in sauce until heated through. Serve at once, with rice.

Serves 4

Stir-fried Chicken with Mangetout

2 tblspn oil

500g (1lb) boneless chicken breasts, skinned and cut in bite-sized pieces

salt

freshly ground black pepper

200g (6 1/2oz) mangetout, topped and tailed

3 tblspn finely grated fresh root ginger

1 clove garlic, finely chopped

75ml (2 1/2fl oz) chicken stock

1 1/2 tblspn soy sauce

2 tblspn chopped fresh coriander

1 Preheat wok, then add oil. When hot, add chicken and stir fry over high heat for 3 minutes. Season with salt and pepper, add mangetout and stir fry for 2 minutes more. Add ginger and garlic and stir fry for 1 further minute.

2 Move mixture to sides of wok and add chicken stock and soy sauce to centre. Heat for 1 minute, then toss with chicken and mangetout. Sprinkle with chopped coriander and serve.

Serves 4

Indonesian Chicken and Green Beans

18

Chicken with Ginger and Peanuts

75ml (2¹/2fl oz) dry white wine

1 tspn finely grated ginger

1 clove garlic, crushed

500g (1lb) boneless chicken breasts, skinned and cut in 2.5cm (1in) cubes

2 tblspn oil

250ml (8fl oz) chicken stock

125g (4oz) crunchy peanut butter

2 spring onions, cut in thin strips

1 red chilli, seeded and sliced

1 Combine wine, ginger and garlic in a large shallow dish. Add chicken cubes and stir to coat. Cover and set aside for 30 minutes. Drain chicken, reserving marinade.

2 Preheat wok, then add oil. When hot, add chicken and stir fry over high heat for 2 minutes until just cooked. Add reserved marinade, stock and peanut butter. Bring to the boil, stirring, then simmer for 5 minutes.

3 Add spring onions and chilli and cook for 1 minute more.
Serves 4

Chicken and Artichoke Stir Fry with Prosciutto

2 tblspn oil

4 boneless chicken breasts, cut in 2cm (³/4in) cubes

1 onion, roughly chopped

1 clove garlic, crushed

200g (6¹/2oz) prosciutto, finely chopped

4 drained canned artichoke hearts, cut in half

90g (3oz) stuffed green olives, cut in half

3 tblspn dry white wine

1 tspn chopped fresh thyme

1 tblspn chopped fresh basil

1 Preheat wok, then add oil. When hot, add chicken and stir fry for 3-4 minutes until cooked. Transfer chicken to a bowl.

Chicken with Ginger and Peanuts

2 Reheat oil in wok. Add onion and garlic and stir fry for 2 minutes. Return chicken to wok and stir in prosciutto, artichoke hearts, olives, wine and herbs. Cook for 2-3 minutes until heated through.
Serves 4

Chicken with Courgettes and Butternut Squash

1 egg white

1 tblspn dry white wine

¹/2 tspn salt

1 tblspn cornflour

4 boneless chicken breasts, skinned and cut in 5mm (¹/4in) strips

2 tblspn oil

1 small onion, finely chopped

2 cloves garlic, crushed

250g (8oz) courgettes, cut in fine strips

250g (8oz) butternut squash, peeled and cut in fine strips

freshly ground black pepper

2 tblspn chopped fresh basil

radicchio leaves to serve

1 Combine egg white, wine, salt and cornflour in a blender and process until smooth. Transfer mixture to a shallow dish, add chicken and stir to coat. Cover and refrigerate for at least 3 hours.

2 Bring a large saucepan of water to the boil, reduce heat to a simmer and stir in chicken. Simmer for 2 minutes or until chicken is almost cooked. Drain, rinse, drain and dry on paper towels.

3 Preheat wok, then add oil. When hot, add onion and stir fry for 1 minute. Add garlic; mix well. Add courgettes and squash and stir fry for 3 minutes. Add chicken and toss with vegetables until heated. Season with pepper, add basil and toss well. Cool slightly. Serve on a bed of radicchio leaves.
Serves 4

Chicken Stroganoff

Chicken Stroganoff

60g (2oz) butter, see Kitchen Tip

1 tblspn oil

500g (1lb) boneless chicken breasts, skinned and cut in thin strips

155g (5oz) mushrooms, halved

125ml (4fl oz) dry white wine

250ml (8fl oz) double cream

2 tblspn tomato puree

1/2 tspn grated nutmeg

1 tblspn finely chopped spring onions

spring onion green for garnish

1 Melt half the butter in the oil in a wok over moderate heat. Add the chicken strips and stir fry for about 3 minutes until tender and cooked through. Using a slotted spoon, transfer to a bowl and set aside.

2 Add the remaining butter to the wok. When melted, add the mushrooms and cook over moderate heat for 1 minute. Stir in wine, cream, tomato puree and nutmeg and cook over high heat for 5 minutes or until sauce thickens slightly.

3 Return the chicken to the wok, toss in the sauce and heat through for 1-2 minutes. Stir in spring onions and serve at once, garnished with spring onion green.
Serves 4

Kitchen Tip
Although butter is not generally used in wok cookery its flavour is essential for this dish. Adding oil helps to prevent it from burning, but it is nonetheless recommended that only moderate heat be used for the preliminary frying.

Honey Soy Sauce Chicken Wings

2 tblspn oil

1 clove garlic, crushed

1 tblspn grated fresh root ginger

8 chicken wings

60ml (2fl oz) Worcestershire sauce

3 tblspn honey

3 tblspn soy sauce

3 tblspn sesame seeds

1 Preheat wok, then add oil. Heat gently, then add garlic and ginger and stir fry for 1 minute until fragrant.

2 Add the chicken wings to the wok and stir fry for 3 minutes.

3 Stir in the Worcestershire sauce honey, and soy sauce. Cook for about 5 minutes until the sauce thickens and coats the chicken wings. Check that the chicken wings are cooked through.

4 Stir in the sesame seeds, mix well and serve.
Serves 4

Chicken Teriyaki with Yogurt Chilli Sauce

3 tblspn light soy sauce

3 tblspn Worcestershire sauce

2 tblspn red wine vinegar

60ml (2fl oz) pale dry sherry

2 tblspn brown sugar

2 cloves garlic, crushed

500g (1lb) boneless chicken breasts, skinned and cut in thin strips

2 tblspn oil

1 x 185g (6oz) can pimientos, drained and sliced

1 tblspn cornflour

Yogurt Sauce

155ml (5fl oz) low fat natural yogurt

1 tblspn freshly squeezed lime juice

1 tspn sweet chilli sauce, or to taste

1 Mix soy sauce, Worcestershire sauce, vinegar, sherry, brown sugar and garlic and pour into a large shallow dish. Add chicken and stir to coat. Refrigerate, covered, for several hours. Drain chicken, reserving marinade.

2 Make yogurt sauce by mixing all ingredients in a bowl. Set aside.

3 Preheat wok, then add oil. When hot, add chicken and stir fry over high heat for 3 minutes. Add pimientos and stir fry for 2 minutes.

4 Stir cornflour into reserved marinade, add mixture to the wok and cook, stirring, until the sauce thickens. Serve with sauce.
Serves 4

Chicken with Mushrooms and Fresh Herbs

2 tblspn oil

500g (1lb) boneless chicken breasts, skinned and cut in thin strips

2 leeks, thinly sliced

125g (4oz) mushrooms, sliced

90g (3oz) drained bottled sun-dried tomatoes, sliced

2 tblspn red wine vinegar

3 tblspn freshly squeezed lime juice

1/2 tspn finely chopped red chilli

1 tblspn chopped fresh basil

1 tblspn chopped parsley

1 Preheat wok, then add oil. When hot, add chicken and stir fry over high heat for 3 minutes. Transfer chicken to a bowl and set aside.

2 Reheat oil in wok, add leeks, mushrooms and sun-dried tomatoes and stir fry for 2 minutes.

3 Add vinegar, lime juice, chilli and fresh herbs. Bring to the boil, then simmer until sauce thickens slightly. Return chicken to wok, toss in sauce and heat through for 1-2 minutes. Serve at once.
Serves 4

Chicken with Mushrooms and Fresh Herbs

Chicken with Peanut Satay Sauce

2 tblspn oil

500g (1lb) boneless chicken breasts, skinned and cut in thin strips

90g (3oz) smooth peanut butter

60ml (2fl oz) water

3 tblspn pale dry sherry

2 tspn grated fresh root ginger

1 clove garlic, crushed

60g (2oz) peanuts

1 tspn ground cumin

125ml (4fl oz) coconut milk

2 tblspn freshly squeezed lime juice

1 tspn mild curry powder

1 tblspn fruit chutney

1 tblspn honey

1 Preheat wok, then add oil. When hot, add chicken strips and stir fry over high heat for 3 minutes. Using a slotted spoon, transfer chicken to a dish and set aside.

2 Pour off all but 1 tspn of oil from the wok. Combine the peanut butter, water, sherry, ginger, garlic, peanuts, cumin, coconut milk, lime juice, curry powder, chutney and honey in a blender or food processor and process until ingredients are combined and peanuts are finely chopped. Pour into wok, bring to the boil, then simmer for 5 minutes, stirring constantly.

3 Return chicken strips to the wok and cook over moderate heat, stirring until coated in the sauce and heated through.
Serves 4

QUICK FISH DISHES FROM THE WOK

Fish is the original fast food. It requires no elaborate preparation and cooks to perfection in a very short time, two characteristics that make it a classic candidate for the wok. Seafood such as prawns and octopus, and fish such as John Dory are particularly suited to this cooking method, as the recipes that follow illustrate.

John Dory and Vegetable Stir Fry

(Illustrated on pages 42-43)

250g (8oz) broccoli

3 tblspn oil

500g (1lb) John Dory fillets, skinned and cut in strips

1 onion, cut in quarters, then separated into petals

1/2 red pepper, cut in thin strips

90g (3oz) bamboo shoots, cut in thin strips or 4 yellow squash (custard marrows), sliced

1 tspn sugar

125ml (4fl oz) light fish or vegetable stock

2 tspn chilli sauce

1 Cut off the broccoli florets and set aside. Cut the broccoli stems diagonally in 2cm (3/4in) slices.

2 Preheat wok, then add oil. When hot, add the fish strips in small batches and stir fry over moderate heat for 2-3 minutes, taking care not to stir the fish so vigorously that it breaks up. Using a slotted spoon, transfer the fish to a dish and set aside.

3 Reheat the oil in the wok, add the broccoli stems, onion, pepper and bamboo shoots or squash and stir fry for 3 minutes over high heat.

4 Add the broccoli florets and stir fry for 1 minute. Stir in the sugar, stock and chilli sauce, bring to the boil, then return the fish to the wok and simmer, turning carefully once or twice, until coated in the sauce and heated through. Serve at once.

Serves 4

Spicy Prawns with Sun-dried Tomatoes

3 tblspn oil

1kg (2lb) uncooked king prawns, peeled and deveined, tails intact

1 tblspn tomato puree

2 tspn brown sugar

2 cloves garlic, crushed

1 tblspn chilli sauce

1 tblspn chopped fresh coriander

140g (4^1/$_2$oz) bottled sun-dried tomatoes, drained

1 tblspn freshly squeezed lime juice

fresh herbs for garnish

1 Preheat wok, then add oil. When hot, add the prawns and stir fry over high heat for about 2 minutes until cooked. Using a slotted spoon, transfer prawns to a dish and set aside.

Spicy Prawns with Sun-dried Tomatoes

2 Pour off all but 1 tspn of oil from the wok. Add the tomato puree, sugar, garlic, chilli sauce and coriander. Bring to the boil, then simmer for 1 minute.

3 Stir in the sun-dried tomatoes and lime juice. Return the prawns to the wok, turn to coat in the sauce and heat through. Serve at once, garnished with fresh herbs.
Serves 4

Kitchen Tip
To peel a prawn, first break off the head and discard it. Hold the prawn so that the underside is uppermost and pull the shell apart. Slip the shell off, either leaving the tail intact, as for the recipe above, or breaking it off.

Sweet Soy Octopus

1kg (2lb) baby octopus
1 tblspn sunflower oil
1 tblspn sesame oil
2 tblspn clear honey
3 tblspn Worcestershire sauce
2 cloves garlic, crushed
1 tblspn tomato puree
60ml (2fl oz) soy sauce
2 tblspn water
1 tblspn finely snipped fresh chives for garnish

1 Discard heads and beaks of octopus, rinse, drain and dry on paper towels.

2 Preheat wok, then add oils and honey. Stir over moderate heat for 30 seconds, then add Worcestershire sauce, garlic, tomato puree, soy sauce and water. Bring to the boil, then simmer until the sauce thickens.

3 Add the prepared octopus and cook over moderate heat for 2 minutes or until cooked through, turning to coat the octopus in the sauce.

4 Serve at once, garnished with chives.

Serves 4

Sweet Soy Octopus

Quick Fry Prawn Curry

1 tblspn sunflower oil
1 tblspn sesame oil
1 large onion, chopped
2 sticks celery, diagonally sliced
2 red peppers, cut in 1cm (1/2in) cubes
1 1/2 tblspn mild curry powder
1 cucumber, peeled and chopped, see Kitchen Tip
1 x 440g (14oz) can peeled tomatoes
250ml (8fl oz) chicken stock
750g (1 1/2lb) uncooked or cooked prawns, peeled and deveined
22g (3/4oz) unsweetened desiccated coconut
1 tblspn lemon juice
salt
freshly ground black pepper

1 Preheat wok, then add oils. When hot, add onion, celery and peppers and stir fry over high heat for 3 minutes.

2 Stir in curry powder and cook over moderate heat for 1 minute, then add cucumber and stir fry for 2 minutes.

3 Add tomatoes and stock. Bring to the boil, then reduce heat to a simmer. Add prawns. Simmer uncooked prawns for 3-5 minutes until cooked; if using cooked prawns, just heat through.

4 Remove wok from heat, add coconut and lemon juice and stir lightly. Add salt and pepper to taste and serve at once.
Serves 6

Kitchen Tip
To prepare the peeled cucumber, cut it lengthwise in quarters, cut away the seeds with a sharp knife, then slice the firm flesh diagonally in small crescent shapes.

Stir-fried Scallops in White Wine

Cooking Fish in the Wok

The firmer types of fish and seafood can be cooked quickly and with considerable success in the wok. John Dory, plaice, sole, haddock, prawns and scallops are all suitable, but because fish is not as robust as meat, greater care must be taken not to break up the pieces when stirring. The technique resembles deep frying in that slightly more oil than usual is used, with the fish cooked in batches if necessary to avoid crowding the wok.

Whole fish, provided it is of suitable size, can also be steamed on a rack over boiling water or stock in a wok. Grey mullet, whiting, sole, plaice and trout, either whole or in one piece, are all suitable. The fish should be cleaned and scaled, but not filleted or skinned. A 750g (1½lb) fish will require 15-20 minutes.

Stir-fried Scallops in White Wine

3 tblspn oil
250g (8oz) shelled scallops
60ml (2fl oz) white wine
250ml (8fl oz) double cream
pinch thyme
2 tblspn finely snipped chives
dill sprig for garnish

1 Preheat wok, then add oil. When hot, add scallops and stir fry over moderate heat for 1-2 minutes or until cooked through but still tender. Using a slotted spoon, transfer scallops to a bowl and set aside.

2 Pour off all but 1 tspn of oil from the wok. Add the wine, cream and thyme and bring to the boil, then simmer for about 6 minutes or until slightly reduced.

3 Return scallops to pan, turn to coat in the sauce and reheat.
Serves 2

Prawns in Yogurt

2 tblspn oil
1 small onion, chopped
¼ tspn turmeric
2 tblspn ground coriander
750g (1½lb) uncooked prawns, peeled and deveined
salt
freshly ground black pepper
cayenne pepper to taste
60ml (2fl oz) natural low fat yogurt mixed with 1 tblspn flour
125ml (4fl oz) water

1 Preheat wok, then add oil. When hot, add the onion, turmeric and coriander and stir fry over high heat for 2 minutes.

2 Add the prawns and stir fry for 2 minutes until cooked. Season with salt, pepper and cayenne.

3 Stir in the yogurt mixture and water. Cook, stirring, until sauce thickens. Stir to ensure that prawns are well coated.
Serves 4

Seafood Stir Fry

2 tblspn oil
2 small onions, chopped
1 small green pepper, chopped
1 small red pepper, chopped
2 cloves garlic, crushed
2 tomatoes, chopped
250ml (8fl oz) water
150ml (5fl oz) dry white wine
60ml (2fl oz) brandy
1/4 tspn saffron powder
2 bay leaves
1 frozen uncooked lobster tail, thawed, flesh removed from shell and cut into large chunks
500g (1lb) uncooked king prawns in the shell, cleaned
2 tblspn chopped fresh parsley for garnish

1 Preheat wok, then add oil. When hot, add onions, peppers and garlic and stir fry over high heat for 3 minutes.

2 Add tomatoes, lower the heat and simmer for 5 minutes. Mix water, wine, brandy and saffron in a jug, then add to wok with bay leaves. Bring to the boil, then reduce the heat to a simmer.

3 Add the seafood and cook gently for about 5 minutes, until tender. Serve at once, garnished with parsley.
Serves 4

Kitchen Tips
Saffron threads may be used instead of powder, if preferred: Put 1/2 tspn saffron threads in a mortar and pound to a paste with a pestle. Stir in a little boiling water to dissolve the threads, then add to the wok with the remaining water,

wine and brandy.

If cooked lobster and prawns are used, add them right at the end of cooking, tossing them in the sauce until heated through.

Prawn and Mangetout Salad with Sweet Chilli Sauce

185ml (6fl oz) sweet white wine
1 tblspn lemon juice
1 tblspn freshly squeezed lime juice
1 tspn sugar
1 tspn chilli paste or 2 tspn chilli sauce
1 tspn crushed black peppercorns
1/2 tspn ground coriander
315g (10oz) shelled scallops
315g (10oz) uncooked king prawns, peeled and deveined, tails intact
75g (2 1/2oz) mangetout, topped and tailed
2 tblspn oil
1 tblspn chopped fresh parsley

1 Combine the wine, lemon juice, lime juice, sugar, chilli paste or sauce, pepper and coriander in a wok. Bring to the boil over moderate heat.

2 Lower the heat to a simmer, add the scallops and prawns and cook for about 4 minutes until tender. Using a slotted spoon, transfer the seafood to a dish and set aside.

3 Add the mangetout to the wine mixture in the wok and simmer for 1 minute, remove with a slotted spoon and add to the seafood in the dish.

4 Stir the oil and parsley into the wok, cook for 1 minute, then pour over the seafood mixture. Toss well. Cool, then cover and chill until ready to serve.
Serves 4

Prawn and Mangetout Salad with Sweet Chilli Sauce

STIR FRIES WITHOUT MEAT

Healthy eating means cutting down on meat and animal products, and many families now make a conscious effort to have several meat-free meals every week. The simple solution is to serve a stir fry, using the best produce the garden, the greengrocer or the supermarket can supply.

Fruity Bean Stir Fry

salt

315g (10oz) broad beans

1 tblspn oil

1 red onion, sliced

2 carrots, thinly sliced

250ml (8fl oz) apple cider

1 tblspn chopped fresh basil

90g (3oz) drained canned pineapple chunks

90g (3oz) seedless black grapes

1 Bring a saucepan of lightly salted water to the boil, add the broad beans and cook for 7 minutes or until tender. Drain, refresh under cold water, drain again and set aside.

2 Preheat wok, then add oil. When hot, add onion and carrots and stir fry over high heat for 3 minutes. Lower the heat to moderate, add cider and basil and cook for 3-5 minutes until carrot is tender but retains some crunch.

3 Stir in the pineapple and grapes and cook for 2 minutes more.

4 Return the beans to the wok and heat through. Serve hot or cold.
Serves 4

Pawpaw and Vegetable Stir Fry

2 tblspn oil

2 sticks celery, diagonally sliced

1 red onion, sliced

1 leek, cut in thin strips

3 tblspn red wine vinegar

1/4 tspn crushed black peppercorns

1/2 pawpaw, seeded, peeled and sliced

1 tblspn chopped fresh parsley or coriander

cooked brown rice to serve

1 Preheat wok, then add oil. When hot, add celery, onion and leek and stir fry over high heat for 2 minutes. Add vinegar and pepper and stir fry for 1 minute more.

2 Add the pawpaw and parsley and cook for 1 minute more, turning the pawpaw carefully to coat it in the sauce without allowing it to disintegrate. Serve on a bed of brown rice.
Serves 4

Kitchen Tips
Pawpaw, also known as papaya, is a delicious oval fruit with deep yellow skin when ripe and orange or pink flesh. It bruises easily so should be handled with care. To prepare, cut the pawpaw in half, scoop out the grey-black seeds and peel off the skin.

Brown rice, with its nutty flavour, is a good accompaniment for stir fries. A mixture of wild rice and brown rice may also be used.

Pawpaw and Vegetable Stir Fry (top), Fruity Bean Stir Fry

Thai Vegetable Stir Fry

Vegetarians may substitute soy sauce for the fish sauce.

| 1 tspn cornflour |
| 1 tblspn pale dry sherry |
| 125ml (4fl oz) vegetable stock |
| 1/2 tspn sesame oil |
| 1 tblspn fish sauce (nam pla) |
| 1 tblspn sunflower oil |
| 1 carrot, cut in thin strips |
| 3 spring onions, diagonally sliced |
| 125g (4oz) green beans, diagonally sliced |
| 6 fresh asparagus spears, diagonally sliced in 5cm (2in) lengths |
| 60g (2oz) mangetout |
| 1 tspn grated fresh root ginger |
| 60g (2oz) beansprouts |

1 Combine cornflour, sherry, stock, sesame oil and fish sauce. Set aside.

2 Preheat wok, then add sunflower oil. When hot, add carrot, spring onions, beans, asparagus, mangetout and ginger and stir fry over high heat for 2 minutes. Add beansprouts and stir fry for 1 minute.

3 Push vegetables to sides of wok, add cornflour mixture to the centre and bring to the boil, stirring. Toss with the vegetables until well coated.
Serves 4

Squash with Sun-dried Tomatoes

| 6 bottled sun-dried tomatoes, drained (3 tblspn oil reserved) and cut in thin strips |
| 6 pattypan squash (custard marrows), cut in 5mm (1/4in) slices |
| 3 small courgettes, cut in 5mm (1/4in) slices |
| 1 tblspn chopped fresh rosemary |

1 Preheat wok, then add the oil from the sun-dried tomatoes. When hot, add the pattypan squash and courgettes and stir fry over high heat for 2 minutes.

Thai Vegetable Stir Fry

2 Add tomato strips and rosemary, season to taste, toss lightly until heated through.
Serves 4

Kitchen Tip
Pattypans are small round squash with distinctive scalloped edges. Like courgettes, they are summer squash, eaten when the skin is still soft. It is not necessary to remove the skin before cooking.

Stir-fried Broccoli with Pimientos

| 2 tblspn groundnut oil |
| 375g (12oz) broccoli, cut into florets, stems cut diagonally into 2cm (3/4in) slices |
| 90g (3oz) drained canned pimientos, cut in strips |
| 60g (2oz) peanuts |
| 1 tblspn lemon juice |
| 1 tblspn chopped fresh coriander |

1 Preheat wok, then add oil. When hot, add broccoli stems and stir fry over high heat for 2 minutes. Add broccoli florets and stir fry for 1 minute.

2 Add the pimientos, peanuts, lemon juice and coriander, toss over high heat until heated.
Serves 4

Grated Courgette Stir Fry

| 1 tblspn sunflower oil |
| 1 tblspn sesame oil |
| 1 small onion, finely chopped |
| 1/4 tsp grated nutmeg |
| 3 large courgettes, grated |

1 Preheat wok, then add oils. When hot, add onion and stir fry over moderate heat until softened. Do not brown.

2 Stir in nutmeg, then add courgettes and toss over moderate heat for 2-3 minutes until tender.
Serves 4

Stir-fried Chickpeas

1 tblspn cornflour
2 tblspn soy sauce
250ml (8fl oz) water
2 tblspn oil
1 onion, sliced
125g (4oz) Chinese cabbage or Savoy cabbage, shredded
1 green pepper, chopped
2 spring onions, sliced
1 clove garlic, crushed
2 tspn grated fresh root ginger
1 x 440g (14oz) can cooked chickpeas, drained
1 tspn finely grated lemon rind
2 tblspn lemon juice
1/2 tspn ground cumin
pinch chilli powder

1 Mix cornflour, soy sauce and water in a jug and set aside.

2 Preheat wok, then add oil. When hot, add onion, cabbage, green pepper and spring onions. Stir fry over high heat for 2 minutes, then add garlic and ginger and stir fry for 1 minute more.

3 Add the remaining ingredients, with the cornflour mixture and bring to the boil, stirring until the sauce thickens. Reduce the heat and simmer for 3 minutes, then serve.
Serves 4

Carrot and Celery Stir Fry

1 bunch coriander
2 tblspn oil
4 carrots, thinly sliced
3 sticks celery, thinly sliced
1 large leek, thinly sliced
250g (8oz) green beans, diagonally sliced
2 tblspn finely chopped fresh root ginger
2 tblspn light soy sauce
60g (2oz) peanuts

Stir-fried Squash, Mangetout and Red Pepper Strips (top), Stir-fried Vegetables with Ricotta

1 Strip leaves from coriander and set aside for garnish. Chop stems and reserve.

2 Preheat wok, then add oil. When hot, add the carrots, celery, leek, beans, coriander stems and ginger and stir fry over high heat for 3 minutes.

3 Stir in the soy sauce and peanuts and cook for 2 minutes more. Vegetables should be cooked through but still crunchy. Serve at once, garnished with the reserved coriander leaves.
Serves 4

Stir-fried Vegetables with Ricotta

3 tblspn oil
1 aubergine, sliced and chopped
4 courgettes, sliced
200g (6 1/2 oz) pattypan squash (custard marrow), cut in wedges
2 tblspn tarragon vinegar
300g (9 1/2 oz) ricotta cheese

1 Preheat wok, then add oil. When hot, add the aubergine, courgettes and squash and stir fry over high heat for 2 minutes.

2 Add the vinegar, toss with the vegetables and cook for 1 minute more.

3 Spoon a small serving of ricotta onto each plate and serve the vegetable mixture on top.
Serves 4

Stir-fried Squash, Mangetout and Red Pepper Strips

2 tblspn oil
2 red peppers, sliced in thin strips
315g (10oz) yellow squash or courgettes, thinly sliced
155g (5oz) mangetout, topped and tailed
2 tspn finely chopped fresh parsley
2 tspn finely chopped fresh basil
lemon juice

Warm Rice Salad with Peas, Artichokes and Sun-dried Tomatoes

1 Preheat wok, then add oil. When hot, add the pepper strips and stir fry for 1 minute.

2 Add the squash or courgettes and mangetout and stir fry for 2 minutes more.

3 Stir in the parsley and basil, add a squeeze of lemon juice and serve at once.
Serves 4

Tofu Stir Fry

60g (2oz) beansprouts

l tblspn oil

1 clove garlic, crushed

1 tspn grated fresh root ginger

4 spring onions, diagonally sliced

1 small red pepper, cut in thin strips

2 courgettes, sliced

250g (8oz) firm plain or smoked tofu, cut in 2.5cm (1in) cubes

1 tblspn dark soy sauce

1 Put the beansprouts in a heatproof bowl. Pour over boiling water to cover, allow to stand for 2 minutes, then drain. Dry on paper towels.

2 Preheat wok, then add oil. When hot, add garlic, ginger, spring onions, red pepper and courgettes. Stir fry over high heat for 3 minutes.

3 Add beansprouts, tofu and soy sauce, Cook over moderate heat, tossing the ingredients lightly, until heated through. Serve at once.
Serves 4

Tofu

This nutritious ingredient, high in protein but low in fat, has long been a staple food in Asia. The name tofu is used in Japan and Korea; in China it is known as bean curd. It is made from soya beans, which are first softened by soaking in water, then crushed and boiled to create a mixture of pulp and liquid. The liquid – or soya milk – is coagulated to make a thick white paste, which may be smooth and silky (silken tofu) or firm enough to cut.

Thanks to the rapidly increasing popularity of tofu in the West, it is now possible to buy the product in a wide variety of guises. Fresh tofu, packed in brine, is available from many health food shops and Oriental stores, but you can also buy powdered tofu or long-life cartons and packs.

It is the firm tofu (plain, smoked or flavoured) that is of greatest value in wok cookery, as it retains its shape when stir-fried. Silken tofu is used for soups, sauces, dips and even desserts.

Although tofu has little taste of its own, it happily absorbs other flavours and is often marinated before use. It has a particular affinity for ginger, soy sauce and sherry.

Warm Rice Salad with Peas, Artichokes and Sun-dried Tomatoes

1 tblspn oil

2 sticks celery, sliced

60g (2oz) mushrooms, sliced

90g (3oz) yellow squash or courgettes, sliced

60g (2oz) fresh or thawed frozen peas

2 cloves garlic, crushed

45g (1½ oz) drained bottled sun-dried tomatoes, sliced

3 tblspn white wine vinegar

2 tblspn freshly squeezed orange juice

60g (2oz) pawpaw or melon, cut in 1cm (½in) cubes

185g (6oz) drained canned artichoke hearts, halved

250g (8oz) cooked long grain rice

2 large carrots, grated

8 black olives, pitted and halved

flat-leaf parsley for garnish

1 Preheat wok, then add oil. When hot, add celery, mushrooms, squash or courgettes, peas and garlic. Stir fry over high heat for 2 minutes, then add tomatoes and stir fry for 1 minute more.

2 Add the remaining ingredients and toss over heat for 1 minute. Spoon onto a serving dish, garnish with flat-leaf parsley and serve.
Serves 4

Vegetable Strips with Cumin Cream Sauce

2 tblspn oil

2 cloves garlic, halved

1 aubergine, cut in 1 x 5cm (1/2 x 2in) strips

3 carrots, cut in thin strips

1 red pepper, cut in thin strips

5 large mushrooms, cut in strips

2 courgettes, cut in strips

1 tspn ground cumin

1/2 tspn ground coriander

150ml (5fl oz) single cream

150ml (5fl oz) soured cream

1 Preheat wok, then add oil. Heat gently, add garlic and cook for 1 minute. Remove garlic and discard.

2 Add aubergine, carrots and red pepper to wok and stir fry over high heat for 2 minutes. Add mushrooms and courgettes and stir fry for 2 minutes. Transfer to a dish and set aside.

3 Pour off all but 1 tspn of oil from wok. Stir in cumin and coriander and cook for 1 minute over moderate heat, then add the cream and soured cream. Bring to the boil, lower heat and simmer until sauce reduces by half. Return vegetable mixture to wok, toss until heated.
Serves 4

Stir-fried Vegetables with Marinated Tofu

2 tblspn Worcestershire sauce

2 tblspn clear honey

60ml (2fl oz) dark soy sauce

1 tblspn tomato puree

250g (8oz) firm tofu, sliced

1 tblspn oil

4 sticks celery, sliced

2 red peppers, cut in strips

4 courgettes, sliced

Vegetable Strips with Cumin Cream Sauce

1 Combine Worcestershire sauce, soy sauce, honey and tomato puree in a shallow dish. Add tofu, stir gently to coat, cover and marinate in refrigerator for 2 hours.

2 Preheat wok, then add oil. When hot, add tofu, reserving any marinade. Stir fry for 2 minutes over moderate heat. Transfer tofu to a bowl.

3 Add celery, peppers and courgettes to wok and stir fry for 3 minutes, then return the tofu to pan with reserved marinade. Stir over high heat until heated.
Serves 4

Vegetable Risotto

4 tblspn oil

1 onion, chopped

1 clove garlic, crushed

1 carrot, finely chopped

1 tspn ground turmeric

250g (8oz) basmati rice

90ml (3fl oz) dry white wine

1 litre (1 3/4pt) good quality vegetable or chicken stock

125g (4oz) mushrooms, sliced

2 celery sticks, sliced

60g (2oz) broccoli florets

1/2 red pepper, chopped

60ml (2fl oz) double cream

2 tblspn grated Parmesan cheese

1 Preheat wok, then add oil. When hot, add onion, garlic, carrot, turmeric and rice. Stir fry for 2 minutes over moderate heat.

2 Add the wine and stock, bring to the boil, then simmer, stirring occasionally, for 10 minutes.

3 Add the remaining vegetables and cook for 8-10 minutes more over moderate heat until the rice is tender and the stock has almost evaporated.

4 Stir in cream and Parmesan, cook over high heat for 2 minutes, then serve.

Serves 4-6

Hot Lettuce

1 iceberg lettuce

1 tblspn sunflower oil

1 tblspn sesame oil

1 clove garlic, halved

1 tblspn soy sauce

1 tblspn pale dry sherry

1 Separate lettuce leaves. Wash, dry thoroughly on paper towels and tear into large pieces, about 2.5 x 7.5cm (1 x 3in).

2 Preheat wok, then add oils. Heat gentle, then add garlic and cook for 1 minute to flavour oil. Using a slotted spoon, remove garlic and discard.

3 Add lettuce and stir fry over high heat for 2 minutes, turning the lettuce over and moving it about with a spatula rather than a spoon. The lettuce should remain crisp and green.

4 Move the lettuce to the sides of the wok, add the soy sauce and sherry to the centre and cook for 1 minute. Toss the lettuce with the sauce and serve at once.
Serves 4

Variations
Use Cos lettuce, Chinese cabbage, young spinach leaves or spring greens instead of iceburg lettuce, increasing the cooking time to about 4 minutes for cabbage or greens. Oyster sauce may be used instead of soy sauce, and diagonally sliced spring onions added with the sauce and sherry mixture if liked.

Spiced Almonds and Pecans

60ml (2fl oz) groundnut oil

185g (6oz) whole blanched almonds

125g (4oz) pecan nuts

60g (2oz) sugar

1 tspn salt

2 tspn ground cumin

1 tspn chilli powder

1 Heat oil in a wok. Add almonds, pecans and sugar, stirring over moderate heat until almonds are light golden brown.

2 Using a slotted spoon, transfer the nuts to a heatproof bowl. Add salt, cumin and chilli powder and toss well to coat.

3 Cool for at least 10 minutes before serving.
Serves 4-6

Vegetable and Nut Stir Fry

1 tspn turmeric

1 tblspn caster sugar

1 tblspn cider vinegar

1 clove garlic, crushed

2 tblspn vegetable stock

2 tblspn oil

1 onion, quartered, then separated into petals

1 large carrot, cut in thin strips

2 sticks celery, diagonally sliced

4 spring onions, diagonally sliced

125g (4oz) mangetout, topped and tailed

90g (3oz) roasted cashew nuts

1 Mix turmeric, sugar, vinegar, garlic and stock in a small bowl. Set aside.

2 Preheat wok, then add oil. When hot, add onion, carrot and celery and stir fry over high heat for 3 minutes. Add spring onions and mangetout and stir fry for 2 minutes more.

3 Stir in turmeric and stock mixture and cook over moderate heat for 2-3 minutes more, until vegetables are crisp tender and the sauce has thickened slightly. Stir through nuts and serve.
Serves 4

Spiced Almonds and Pecans

Crisp Spring Greens with Almonds

375g (12oz) young spring greens

oil for deep frying

1 tspn caster sugar

½ tspn salt

30g (1oz) flaked almonds

1 Separate spring green leaves. Wash, dry thoroughly on paper towels and shred very finely. Spread out the shreds on paper towels and set aside for 20 minutes to dry completely.

2 Heat the oil for deep frying in the wok (see pages 2-3). Shielding your hand with a cloth, add about a quarter of the shredded spring greens. Reduce the heat to moderate and fry the shreds until they float to the surface, moving them around with a slotted spoon. As soon as they are crisp, transfer them to paper towels to drain. Fry remaining batches in the same way.

3 When the last batch of spring green shreds has been cooked, add the almonds carefully to the hot oil and cook briefly until golden brown. Remove with a slotted spoon and dry on paper towels.

4 Mix the caster sugar and salt together and toss with the fried spring green shreds in a bowl. Top with the almonds and serve.
Serves 4

Kitchen Tip
Watch the almonds constantly when cooking as they burn very readily.

Sweet and Sour Tofu

1 tblspn cornflour

1 tblspn vinegar

75ml (2¹/₂fl oz) water

250ml (8fl oz) pineapple juice

1 tblspn oil

250g (8oz) firm tofu, cut in 2.5cm (1in) cubes

1 red pepper, cut in thin strips

2 carrots, cut in thin strips

155g (5oz) mangetout

2 tspn grated fresh root ginger

1 clove garlic, crushed

185g (6oz) drained canned pineapple chunks

1 Combine cornflour, vinegar, water and pineapple juice. Set aside.

2 Preheat wok, then add oil. When hot, add tofu and stir fry over moderate heat until golden brown. Transfer to a bowl and set aside.

3 Reheat oil in wok, add red pepper, carrots, mangetout, ginger, garlic and pineapple chunks. Stir fry over high heat for 3 minutes.

4 Add cornflour mixture. Bring to the boil, stirring until mixture thickens. Return tofu to wok and turn in sauce until heated.
Serves 4

Vegetable Stir Fry

1 tblspn oil

2 cloves garlic, crushed

2 large carrots, cut in 5cm (2in) matchsticks

2 large courgettes, cut in 5cm (2in) matchsticks

1 parsnip, cut in 5cm (2in) matchsticks

60ml (2fl oz) vegetable stock

2 tbspn snipped fresh chives

1 Preheat wok. Add oil, and when hot, add garlic, carrots, courgettes and parsnip. Stir fry over high heat for 3 minutes.

2 Add stock and chives. Cook for 2-3 minutes.
Serves 4

Hot Sweet and Sour Cucumber Crescents

1 large cucumber

1 tblspn oil

2 tblspn caster sugar

¹/₂ tspn salt

2 tblspn white wine vinegar

2 spring onions, diagonally sliced

1 Top and tail cucumber, cut in half lengthwise, then scoop out seeds. Cut crosswise in 5mm (¹/₄ in) crescents, put in a colander set over a bowl, and sprinkle lightly with salt. Set aside for 20 minutes, then rinse, drain and pat dry.

2 Preheat wok. Add oil and when hot, add sugar, salt and vinegar. Stir fry mixture until it sizzles, add spring onions and cucumber. Stir fry for 2 minutes.
Serves 4

Broccoli and Cauliflower Stir Fry

185g (6oz) broccoli

2 tblspn good quality mayonnaise

2 cloves garlic, crushed

2 tblspn oil

185g (6oz) cauliflower florets

1 Cut off broccoli florets and set aside. Cut broccoli stems diagonally in 2cm (³/₄in) slices.

2 Mix mayonnaise with half the crushed garlic and set aside.

3 Preheat wok, then add oil. When hot, add broccoli stems. Stir fry for 1 minute, then add broccoli and cauliflower florets, and remaining garlic. Stir fry for 2-3 minutes. Serve topped with garlic mayonnaise.
Serves 4

Vegetable Stir Fry

Rice and Noodle Accompaniments

Rice and noodles, whether cooked simply or with additional ingredients, are perfect companions for stir fries, providing contrasts in terms of texture, colour and flavour.

Long-grain rice is usually used for savoury dishes, and should be light and fluffy when cooked. The easiest way to cook rice is by the absorption method. You need twice as much water by volume as rice; the easiest way to measure is by using a cup. For 4 generous portions combine 1¹/₂ cups of long-grain rice and 3 cups of water in a saucepan. Add salt to taste, bring to the boil, stir once, then cover and steam the rice over very low heat until the grains are soft. Easy-cook rice will require about 15 minutes; basmati about 20 minutes, and brown rice 25-35 minutes. The cooking time for brown rice can be reduced if it is first fried in a little butter or oil.

Rice can also be cooked in the oven, as described in the recipe for Persian Rice below. Alternatively, try using the wok to make a creamy risotto, as described on page 35.

Glutinous – or sticky – rice is sometimes served with stir fries. To cook 250g (8oz) glutinous rice, first rinse and drain it thoroughly, then soak it in water to cover for 4 hours. Drain, then put into a saucepan with ¹/₂ tspn salt and 250ml (8fl oz) coconut milk. Add a little lemon grass if liked. Bring to the boil, turn the heat to the lowest setting and cook for about 20 minutes until the liquid has been absorbed. Because the grains stick together, this rice can easily be moulded.

Noodles also make excellent accompaniments for stir fries. Vermicelli and Chinese egg noodles cook very quickly. The best way to achieve good results is to bring a large saucepan of water to the boil, add the noodles, cover the pan and allow it to stand. The noodles will be ready in about 6 minutes – ample time to cook a delicious stir fry!

Rice with Prawns

15g (¹/₂oz) butter
375g (12oz) brown rice
pinch saffron powder dissolved in 750ml (1¹/₄pt) hot chicken or vegetable stock
salt
60ml (2fl oz) French dressing, see Kitchen Tip
1 tblspn snipped chives
¹/₄ tspn mild curry powder
¹/₄ tspn ground cumin
1 tblspn oil
3 spring onions, diagonally chopped
1 red pepper, finely chopped
1 green pepper, finely chopped
500g (1lb) cooked prawns, peeled, deveined and chopped in large pieces

1 Melt the butter in a saucepan over moderate heat, add the rice and cook for 2 minutes, turning to coat the grains thoroughly. Add the saffron and stock mixture, with salt to taste, and bring to the boil. Cook for 5 minutes, lower the heat, cover and steam for about 30 minutes or until the brown rice is tender but still has its 'bite'. Drain the rice if necessary, spoon it into a dish and keep hot until required.

2 Combine dressing, chives, curry powder and cumin in a small jug. Set aside.

3 Preheat wok, then add oil. When hot, add spring onions and peppers and stir fry over high heat for 3 minutes. Add the prawns and stir fry for 1 minute to heat through.

4 Add the prawn mixture to the rice, mix lightly, then add the dressing mixture and toss through. Serve hot or cold.
Serves 4

Kitchen Tip
To make a simple French dressing, combine 3 tblspn olive oil with 1 tblspn wine vinegar. Add salt and freshly ground black pepper to taste. Additional ingredients such as French mustard or soy sauce may be added (the latter would be ideal for the recipe above), and many cooks like to add a pinch of sugar. Make the dressing in a jug or deep bowl, whisking it until the ingredients are well mixed; alternatively, use a screw-topped jar and shake the dressing just before use.

Persian Rice

salt
440g (14oz) basmati rice
2 egg yolks
75g (2¹/₂oz) butter
1 tblspn chopped fresh coriander
1 tspn crushed black peppercorns
75ml (2¹/₂fl oz) water

1 Preheat oven to 180°C (350°F, Gas 4). Bring a saucepan of lightly salted water to the boil. Add the rice and cook for 5 minutes, then drain and transfer to a bowl. Stir in the egg yolks and spoon the mixture into a buttered ovenproof dish.

2 Melt the butter in a small saucepan over moderate heat. Stir in the coriander, pepper and water; pour the mixture over the rice. Bake in the oven for 35 minutes. Serve at once.
Serves 4

Persian Rice is a perfect accompaniment for John Dory and Vegetable Stir Fry (page 24)

Chinese Fried Brown Rice

salt

375g (12oz) long grain brown rice

2 tblspn oil

2 sticks celery, chopped

1 red pepper, chopped

1 clove garlic, crushed

2 eggs, lightly beaten

60g (2oz) cooked peas

4 spring onions, chopped

1 tblspn light soy sauce

1 Bring a large saucepan of lightly salted water to the boil, add the rice and cook for 30-35 minutes until tender. Drain thoroughly, spread rice out on a tray, cool, then refrigerate until cold.

2 Preheat wok, then add the oil. When hot, add the celery, red pepper and garlic and stir fry over high heat for 3 minutes. Using a slotted spoon, transfer to a bowl and set aside.

3 Add the rice to the wok and stir fry until grains are separated. Return the vegetable mixture to the pan with the eggs, peas, spring onions and soy sauce. Cook over moderate heat, stirring until eggs are lightly scrambled and mixture is heated through. Serve at once.
Serves 4

Tofu and Rice Stir Fry

1 tblspn oil

1 onion, chopped

1 carrot, chopped

1 stick celery, chopped

60g (2oz) cauliflower florets

125g (4oz) firm tofu, chopped

1 tblspn dark soy sauce

375g (12oz) cooked brown rice

1 Preheat wok, then add oil. When hot, add onion and stir fry over high heat for 3 minutes. Add remaining vegetables and stir fry for 3 minutes more.

Chinese Fried Brown Rice

2 Push the vegetables to the sides of the wok and add the tofu to the centre. Stir fry for 3 minutes, using a spatula or turner and a gentle action to avoid breaking up the tofu.

3 Lower the heat, add the soy sauce and rice and cook gently, stirring occasionally, until heated through. Serve at once.
Serves 4

Egg-fried Rice

3 tblspn oil

375g (12oz) cooked long grain white rice

60g (2oz) lean cooked roast pork or ham, cut in thin strips

4 spring onions, finely chopped

2 eggs, lightly beaten

1 tblspn light soy sauce

1/4 tspn sugar

freshly ground black pepper

2 tblspn finely chopped fresh coriander

1 Preheat wok, then add oil. When hot, add rice and stir fry over moderate heat for about 3 minutes or until pale gold in colour and free from lumps.

2 Add pork or ham and spring onions and stir fry for 2 minutes more.

3 Push the rice and other ingredients to the sides of the wok and add the beaten eggs to the centre. Stir until lightly scrambled, then mix with rice, pork or ham and spring onions.

4 Stir in soy sauce, sugar, black pepper and coriander. Serve at once.
Serves 4

Kitchen Tip
Cook the rice for this dish the day before using, if possible. When cool, cover and refrigerate until required.

Stir-fried Noodles

250g (8oz) medium egg noodles
3 tblspn oil
1 clove garlic, halved
500g (1lb) uncooked prawns, peeled and deveined
2 tblspn soy sauce
1 tblspn white vinegar
1 tblspn brown sugar
185g (6oz) beansprouts
4 spring onions, cut in short lengths

1 Bring a large saucepan of salted water to the boil, add the egg noodles, remove from the heat and allow to stand for about 6 minutes until noodles are tender or *al dente*. Drain thoroughly. The noodles should be dry but not stiff.

2 Preheat wok, then add oil. Heat gently, then add garlic and stir fry for 1 minute to flavour oil.

3 Add prawns to wok and stir fry over high heat for 2 minutes, then add noodles, soy sauce, vinegar and brown sugar. Toss over high heat for 1 minute.

4 Push the ingredients in the wok to the sides and add the beansprouts and spring onions to the centre. Stir fry for 1 minute, toss with noodle mixture and serve at once.
Serves 4

Oriental Noodles

625g (1¼lb) fresh thin rice noodles, see Kitchen Tip
3 tblspn oil
1 large onion, chopped
90g (3oz) rindless streaky bacon, cut in thin strips
2 tblspn pale dry sherry
I clove garlic, crushed
125g (4oz) beansprouts
2 sticks celery, finely chopped
3 spring onions, chopped
1 tblspn light soy sauce
1 tblspn dark soy sauce

1 Soak the noodles in hot (not boiling) water for 1 minute to soften. Drain thoroughly, dry on paper towels, then cut noodles in thin strips.

2 Preheat wok, then add 2 tablespoons of the oil. When hot, add onion and bacon and stir fry over high heat for 3 minutes until bacon is crisp and onions lightly browned.

3 Add sherry and garlic and stir fry for I minute, then add beansprouts, celery and spring onions and stir fry for 2 minutes more. Using a slotted spoon, transfer the vegetables to a bowl and set aside.

4 Add the remaining oil to the wok. When hot, add noodles and stir gently until heated through. Return the vegetable mixture to the pan with the soy sauces and toss lightly until well combined and hot. Serve.
Serves 4

Kitchen Tip
Fresh rice noodles can be obtained from Oriental food stores.

Cellophane Noodle Salad

315g (10oz) cellophane noodles
1 large carrot, very finely chopped
5 spring onions, very finely chopped
1 tblspn sesame oil
1 tblspn white wine vinegar
2 tblspn freshly squeezed lime juice

1 Put the noodles in a large bowl with hot water to cover. Soak for about 30 minutes or until softened, then drain well.

2 Mix the carrot, spring onions, sesame oil, vinegar and lime juice in a salad bowl, add the noodles and toss well.
Serves 4

Cellophane Noodle Salad is delicious with Heavenly Beef and Vegetables (page 13).

MENUS FOR WOK MEALS

As you become a confident wok cook, you may well wish to prepare entire meals using this marvellous utensil. You may even be tempted to buy another wok or two – one famous cook is reputed to have eight – but there's no real need to do this. Provided all your preparation is done in advance, most of the dishes in this book can be cooked in minutes, and those cooked first will not suffer from being kept warm for the brief time it takes to cook successive dishes.

A wok meal is a friendly affair and the best way of ensuring that your guests develop healthy appetites is to involve them in the process. Let them help with the preparation and enjoy the delectable aromas as you impress them with your cooking skills.

The dishes on the menus that follow are all drawn from the book. Most dishes, when accompanied by a noodle or rice dish, will serve 4 persons, but it is usual to allow rather more food when entertaining, and menus suggest several dishes. Adjust the quantities according to the number of guests expected.

It is not usual to serve elaborate desserts after wok meals; however, a beautifully arranged platter of fresh fruits would be appropriate, as would a simple sorbet. Alternatively, follow the Chinese tradition and serve tea.

CHILDREN'S CHOICE
Omit the yogurt and chilli sauce with the chicken teriyaki if serving this menu to young children; teenagers, however, tend to enjoy it very much.

Sweet and Sour Meatballs
(page 7)
Burghul (Kitchen Tip, page 10)
Chicken Teriyaki with Yogurt Chilli
Sauce (page 22)
Grated Courgette Stir Fry
(page 31)

FINGER SUPPER
San Choy Bow (page 14)
Chicken in Lettuce (page 16)
Honey Soy Sauce Chicken Wings
(page 22)
Spiced Almonds and Pecans
(page 36)

QUICK AND EASY
Twice-cooked Pork with Noodles
(page 10)
Stir-fried Broccoli with Pimientos
(page 31)
Boiled Rice (page 41)

SALAD DAYS
Warm Steak Salad with Pawpaw
(page 12)
Warm Rice Salad with Peas,
Artichokes and Sun-dried
Tomatoes (page 33)
Cellophane Noodle Salad
(page 44)

WINTER WARMER
Fruity Bean Stir Fry (page 29)
Moroccan Sweet and Spicy Stew
(page 10)
Hot Lettuce (page 36)
Chinese Fried Brown Rice
(page 43)

SIMPLE SUPPER
Vegetable Risotto (page 35)
Glazed Beef Slices with Sesame
Seeds (page 12)

ORIENTAL BANQUET
Stir-fried Scallops in White Wine
(page 26)
Stir-fried Chicken with Cashews
(page 17)
Chinese Ginger Beef (page 6)
Stir-fried Pork with Beans and
Sesame Seeds (page 10)
Egg-fried Rice (page 43)
Crisp Spring Greens with
Almonds (page 37)
Soup (optional)

VEGETARIAN MEAL
In the recipes that follow, substitute soy sauce for Worcestershire sauce and for a vegetarian meal omit the bacon in the Oriental Noodles.

Stir-fried Vegetables with
Marinated Tofu (page 35) or
Sweet and Sour Tofu (page 38)
Crisp Spring Greens with
Almonds (page 37)
Oriental Noodles (page 44)
Plain Boiled Rice (page 40)

GLOSSARY

Most of the ingredients used in this book can readily be found in any large supermarket, delicatessen or Oriental food store.

Bamboo Shoots
Widely used throughout Asia, young bamboo shoots are available canned, either sliced or in large chunks. Any shoots not used immediately can be stored in cold water in the refrigerator for up to a week. The water should be changed daily.

Bean Curd
See Tofu

Bean Sauce
See Black Bean Sauce

Beansprouts
Fresh beansprouts are widely available. Mung beans are usually used for sprouting, but soya beans, adzuki beans and alfalfa seeds are also used, as are the seeds of various grains. To sprout your own dried mung beans, place them in a clean glass jar so that the jar is no more than one-sixth full. Cover the jar with a circle of cheesecloth or muslin, holding it in place with a rubber band. Fill the jar with cold water, swirl it around, then drain off the water. Store in a cool dark place, rinsing the beans with fresh water every day. They should sprout within 2-3 days and be ready to eat in about 5 days.

Bean Thread Noodles
See Cellophane Noodles

Black Bean Sauce
Widely used in China, this is a thick paste which is made from ground soya beans mixed with flour and spices. It is available in jars and cans. Refrigerate after opening. A yellow variety is also available.

Cellophane Noodles
Also known as Bean Thread Noodles, these are fine strands of pasta generally made from bean flour. The name derives from the fact that they are almost transparent when ready for use. Available dried. Preparation often consists simply of soaking in hot water for 30 minutes, but check package instructions.

Chilli Sauce
Sold in bottles, this is a very hot mixture of chillies, vinegar and salt. It should be used with caution. A milder Sweet Chilli Sauce is also available.

Chinese Cabbage
This long cylindrical cabbage resembles Cos lettuce in shape. The leaves are pale green with creamy-white spines. Crisp and delicately flavoured, it is used in salads, stir fries and as a vegetable.

Chinese Dried Mushrooms
Usually dried shiitake mushrooms, these should be soaked for 20 minutes in warm water, then drained and squeezed dry. The tough stem is discarded and the cap is usually sliced before being used in soups, stir fries or braised dishes.

Chinese Ham
A dark red, well-aged ham which is similar to Westphalian ham or prosciutto.

Fish Sauce
Also known as Nam Pla or 'patis', this is a thin brown sauce made from salted and fermented anchovies. It is widely used in Southeast Asia and is a staple ingredient in Thai cooking. There is no substitute.

Five Spice Powder
The 'five spices' of the title can vary, but the most common mixture is cinnamon, star anise, cloves, fennel and Szechuan pepper. Cinnamon, ginger, cloves and nutmeg may also be used. A pungent mixture which gives a delicate but distinctive flavour.

Hoisin Sauce
This thick reddish brown sauce is sold in bottles, cans and jars. It is made from soya beans, sugar, flour, vinegar, salt, chilli, garlic and oil. It gives a sharp sweet and spicy flavour to foods and is frequently used for marinating items such as spareribs. Also known as barbecue sauce.

Lemon Grass
Fresh stems of this aromatic herb are sometimes available in Oriental markets. To use, bruise the stalk and remove from the dish before serving, or chop and slice the lower stem for adding to a dish. The dried herb is known as serai powder; 1 teaspoon is equivalent to 1 stem of lemon grass.

Nam Pla
See Fish Sauce

Oyster Sauce
A thick brown liquid made from oyster juices, water, sugar, salt and starch, this imparts a rich, savoury flavour. It is sold in bottles and cans and is frequently thinned for use with sherry or soy sauce. Refrigerate after opening.

Plum Sauce
Made from Chinese plums, chillies and ginger, with vinegar and sugar, this is a delicious sweet sauce that resembles chutney. It can be used on its own, with cold meats, but is also used in marinades, dips, stir fries and as a filling for meatballs.

Rice Wine
There are many varieties of this wine. Pale dry sherry, while not as potent, may be used as a substitute.

Soy Sauce
Several types of this popular sauce, made from fermented soya beans, are available. Light soy sauce is more delicate than the richer tasting dark soy sauce, while Japanese shoyu has a distinctively different taste.

Star Anise
As its name suggests, this is a star-shaped spice, with a flavour of anise.

Tofu
Bean curd. For more information on this highly nutritious ingredient, see page 33.

Water Chestnuts
Not nuts at all, but walnut-sized bulbs which grow in water. Fresh water chestnuts are not readily available except from specialist Oriental markets, but cans of various sizes are sold in most supermarkets. These are particularly valuable ingredients because they remain crunchy even after prolonged cooking.

INDEX

Beef in Black Bean Sauce 6
Broccoli and Cauliflower Stir Fry 38
Carrot and Celery Stir Fry 32
Cellophane Noodle Salad 44
Chicken and Artichoke Stir Fry with Prosciutto 21
Chicken in Lettuce 16
Chicken Livers with Ginger 18
Chicken Stroganoff 22
Chicken Teriyaki with Yogurt Chilli Sauce 22
Chicken with Courgettes and Butternut Squash 21
Chicken with Ginger and Peanuts 21
Chicken with Mushrooms and Fresh Herbs 23
Chicken with Peanut Satay Sauce 23
Chinese Beef Stir Fry 6
Chinese Fried Brown Rice 43
Chinese Ginger Beef 6
Crisp Spring Greens with Almonds 36
Crunchy Pork and Vegetable Stir Fry 4
Egg-fried Rice 43
Fillet of Pork with Star Anise 4
Fruity Bean Stir Fry 29
Glazed Beef Slices with Sesame Seeds 12
Grated Courgette Stir Fry 31

Heavenly Beef and Vegetables 13
Honey Pork with Vegetable Strips 8
Honey Soy Sauce Chicken Wings 22
Hot Lettuce 36
Hot Sweet and Sour Cucumber Crescents 38
Indonesian Chicken and Green Beans 18
John Dory and Vegetable Stir Fry 24
Lamb Stir Fry with Walnuts 8
Liver Stir Fry in Tomato Sauce 14
Mango and Beef Stir Fry 15
Moroccan Sweet and Spicy Stew 10
Oriental Noodles 44
Pawpaw and Vegetable Stir Fry 29
Peas with Prosciutto and Pinenuts 12
Persian Rice 40
Pork and Sage Stir Fry 8
Prawn and Mangetout Salad with Sweet Chilli Sauce 27
Prawns in Yogurt 26
Quick Fry Prawn Curry 25
Red Cabbage and Beef Stir Fry 14
Rice with Prawns 41
San Choy Bow 14
Seafood Stir Fry 27
Spiced Almonds and Pecans 36
Spicy Prawns with Sun-dried Tomatoes 24
Squash with Sun-dried Tomatoes 31
Stir-fried Beef with Broccoli 15

Stir-fried Broccoli with Pimientos 31
Stir-fried Chicken with Cashews 17
Stir-fried Chicken with Mangetout 18
Stir-fried Chickpeas 32
Stir-fried Noodles 44
Stir-fried Pork with Beans and Sesame Seeds 10
Stir-fried Scallops in White Wine 26
Stir-fried Squash, Mangetout and Red Pepper Strips 32
Stir-fried Vegetables with Marinated Tofu 35
Stir-fried Vegetables with Ricotta 32
Sweet and Sour Tofu 38
Sweet Soy Octopus 25
Sweet and Sour Meatballs 7
Tasty Chicken with Peas and Pasta 16
Thai Vegetable Stir Fry 31
Tofu and Rice Stir Fry 43
Tofu Stir Fry 33
Twice-cooked Pork with Noodles 10
Vegetable and Nut Stir Fry 36
Vegetable Risotto 35
Vegetable Stir Fry 38
Vegetable Strips with Cumin Cream Sauce 35
Warm Rice Salad with Peas, Artichokes and Sun-dried Tomatoes 33
Warm Steak Salad with Pawpaw 12

Editorial Coordination: Merehurst Limited
Cookery Editors: Polly Boyd, Jenni Fleetwood, Katie Swallow
Editorial Assistant: Sheridan Packer
Production Manager: Sheridan Carter
Layout and Finished Art: Stephen Joesph
Cover Photography: David Gill
Cover Design: Maggie Aldred

Published by J.B. Fairfax Press Pty Limited
80-82 McLachlan Avenue
Rushcutters Bay 2011
A.C.N. 003 738 430
Formatted by J.B. Fairfax Press Pty Limited
Printed by Toppan Printing Co, Singapore

JBFP 248 A/UK
Includes Index
ISBN 1 86343 117 9
ISBN 1 86343 116 0 (Set)

DISTRIBUTION AND SALES ENQUIRIES
Australia: J.B. Fairfax Press Pty Limited
Ph: (02) 361 6366 Fax: (02) 360 6262
United Kingdom: J.B. Fairfax Press Limited
Ph (0933) 402330 Fax (02) 402234